ID0582230

Pocket
Graces

To my husband Vic,

in gratitude for his love, patience and affirmation

over the years.

G Pocket

Graces

compiled by
Pam Robertson

National Society/Church House Publishing

National Society/Church House Publishing,
Church House, Great Smith Street,
London SW1P 3NZ

ISBN 0 7151 4847 8

First published in 1994 by The National Society and
Church House Publishing

Cover design and illustration by Julian Smith
Text design and typesetting by The National Society

Printed in India by Indeprint Print Production Services
at Thomson Press (India) Ltd.

CONTENTS

Taking the five loaves and the two fish and looking up to heaven, he gave thanks and broke the loaves. Then he gave them to the disciples, and the disciples gave them to the people.

Matthew 14.19

General Graces

General graces

For what we are about to receive
May the Lord make us truly thankful.

We break the bread of brotherhood,
And thank thee, Lord, for all things good.
May we, more blessed than we deserve,
Live less for self, and more to serve. Amen.

God, we thank you for this food.
For rest and home and all things good.
For wind and rain and sun above
But most of all for those we love.

May God bless this food to our use
And ourselves in his service.
For Jesus' sake. Amen.

For good food, good friends and
good fellowship,
We thank you, Lord, in Jesus' name.

Father, as your gospel teaches,
We must love in word and deed.
Bless us gathered round this table
Help us share with those in necd.

For food and friendship day by day,
we bless you, heavenly father.

Lord, for these and all your gifts,
we give you thanks.
In thanks to God for all his benefits
Let us have a moment's silence for the hungry of
the world.

General graces

Bless those that sit at this table, the food that is on it, and those who prepared it. Amen.

Pam Robertson

As we gather in this place,
Brief but heartfelt is our grace:
Thank you, Lord, for friends and food.
Thank you, Lord, for all things good.

Audrey Stanley

O Lord Jesus, Bread of life,
bless this food that it may bring
refreshment to our bodies
and healing to our souls now and for ever.

Heavenly Father,
We thank you for our homes and families,
for our food and clothing, and for all the happiness
that parents and children can share. We ask that
your love may surround us, your care protect us
and that we may know your peace at all times, for
Jesus' sake. Amen.

M H Botting

For these gifts of food and your care day by day,
heavenly father, we thank you. Amen.

F W Street

In giving you thanks for this food, we give you
thanks for all those who have worked so that
we may enjoy it.

General graces

We have food
while others are starving.
We have companions
while others are alone.

May the goodness we receive
strengthen our resolve
to share your blessings
with all your children.

David W Lankshear

Father, we thank thee for the night,
And for the pleasant morning light;
For rest and food and loving care,
And all that makes the day so fair.

Help us to do the things we should,
To be to others kind and good;
In all we do at work or play
To grow more loving every day.

Rebecca J Weston

O give thanks to him who made
Morning light and evening shade.
Source and giver of all good,
Nightly sleep and daily food,
Quickener of our wearied powers
Guard of our unconscious hours.

Josiah Condor (1836)

G racious God, may the food that we are about
to receive strengthen our bodies, and may
thy Holy Spirit strengthen and refresh our souls
through Jesus Christ.

The Tent and the Altar

L ord God, we thank you for all the good things
of your providing, and we pray for the time
when people everywhere shall have the abundant
life of your will, revealed to us in Jesus Christ
your son, our Lord.

Bishop George Appleton (1902-93)

General graces

God, you give good things liberally and judge not. May all who shall eat and drink together at this table be joined in true friendship, and praise you with thankful hearts: through Jesus Christ our Lord.

May God relieve the wants of others and give us thankful hearts: for Christ's sake.

John Dallas

O Lord, give us grateful hearts
For the food now set before us
And supply the wants of others.
For Christ's sake.

Charles Shepherd

Lord, make us thankful, for this food and for all your love, through Jesus Christ our Lord.

O you who clothe the lilies
and feed the birds of the air
Who lead the lambs to pasture
and the hart to the water's side.

Who has multiplied loaves and fishes
and converted water into wine,
Come to our table
as giver and guest to dine.

Stephen Doyle OFM

For food to eat, and those who prepare it,
For health to enjoy it, and friends to share it,
We thank thee, O Lord.

Charles Shepherd

General graces

O Heavenly Father, who by thy blessed son
has taught us to ask of thee our daily bread:
Have compassion on the millions of our fellow
men who live in poverty and hunger; relieve their
distress, make plain the way of help and grant thy
grace unto us all, that we may bear each other's
burdens according to thy will, through Jesus
Christ our Lord.

Bishop George Appleton (1902-93)

F or all the glory of the way.
For thy protection night and day.
For roof-tree, fire, and bed and board
For all thy gifts we thank you, Lord.

The Wayfarers' Grace
M Elizabeth Worsfold

O God, we thank you for the gift of life and for the faculties which enable us to enjoy it. You have given us our eyes to see the beauty of the world, our ears to hear speech and the sound of music, our tongues to taste the good food of your creation, our lips with which to speak in friendship to others and our hands with which to minister to their needs. Help us through the grace of your Holy Spirit, to use all that we have in your service and for your greater glory. Through Jesus Christ our Lord.

General graces

B lessed are you, Lord our God, king of the universe who feeds the entire world in his goodness, with grace, with kindness and with mercy. He gives food to all for his kindness is eternal. Blessed are you, God, who nourishes all.

B lessed art thou, O Lord our God, king of the universe, who bringest forth bread from the earth.

Graces for Organisations

Graces for organisations ———

The Army

Thank you, Lord, for this Mess. Amen.

For good fellowship in freedom,
And for those who made it possible,
We give thanks.

Cecil Hunt

The Navy

No chaplain. Thank God. Amen.

Lord, I've got it down.
You keep it down.

Grace on board ship

God save the King,
Bless our dinners,
Make us thankful.

Admiral Lord Nelson (1758-1805)

Graces for organisations ———

The Air Force

For the spirit of adventure which takes us
into the air,
For the grace of God which brings us
safely back to earth,
For the comradeship which draws us together,
For the blessing of good food,
For these and all his mercies God's holy name
be praised. Amen.

Group Captain E F Haylock, RAF (Retd.)

War Veterans

For valour – a phase so short
 and yet a world of meaning caught
and held for all to learn.

In muddy trench and foreign field
where terror cried, 'it's hopeless, yield!'
quiet hope and courage burned.

In flaming aircraft, sinking wreck,
smoking cockpit, bloodstained deck,
brave hearts and spirits turned.

'Thank God for valour' be our grace.
'For friends in this and every place,
for food and freedom dearly earned.'

*A grace for gatherings of service veterans,
originally written for a lunch for 50 VCs
held at the Royal Tournament*

Patrick Forbes

Graces for organisations ———

Bankers

Father, for money, for pfennigs and francs,
for deutschmarks and sterling
we yield you our thanks.
When equities soar and bulls prowl around
Keep us from greed and our feet on the ground.

Architects and Surveyors

Lord God, survey us with serenity, measure us
with mercy and build us through this feast
into a people fit to please you (and our clients)
now and for ever.

Christopher Herbert

Estate Agents

Dear God, architect of the universe, bless this food to our use and grant us through its nourishment to have a gift with words, an eye for a south-facing aspect and the confidence and humility to meet our clients' every need, now and always. Amen

Christopher Herbert

The Rotary Club

O Lord and giver of all good,
We thank thee for our daily food,
May Rotary aims and Rotary ways
Help us to serve thee all our days.

Graces for organisations ────

The Women's Institute

Thank God for dirty dishes,
 They have a tale to tell.
Whilst other folk go hungry
We've eaten very well.
For home and health, and happiness
We shouldn't make a fuss,
For by this pile of evidence,
God's been very good to us.

Cricketers

O Lord, you'd scarcely think it wicket
   to give you thanks for wondrous cricket,
to celebrate the fans who make
and send those lovely gifts of cake.
Now shades of that great Grace attend
to take guard at the gasworks end
and praise with us the life of Brian
whose commentaries we all rely on.
Give thanks to God, you cricket lovers,
for food and drink. Remove the covers!

A grace written to mark a birthday celebration in honour of the late Brian Johnstone's 80th birthday

Patrick Forbes

Graces for organisations ———

Girl Guides

For food in a world where many walk in hunger;
For faith in a world where many walk in fear;
For friends in a world where many walk alone,
We give you humble thanks, O Lord.

'World Hunger Grace'
Girl Guides of Canada

The Scouts

For food, for clothing, for friendship for
scouting,
Lord we thank you.

Humorous
Graces

Humorous graces ———————

For every cup and plate full,
May the Lord God make us grateful.

God bless this bunch as they munch
their lunch.

I'm ready for it, Lord,
and it's ready for me!

For porridge and for buttered toast
Praise Father Son and Holy Ghost.

H Ingamells

This is the day the Lord has made
Thank you for the toast and marmalade.

For cabbage, corn and shepherds pie.
We praise the Lord who dwells on high.

H Ingamells

For well-filled plate
And brimming cup
And freedom from the washing up.
We thank you, Lord. Amen.

Humorous graces ───────

L ord, as we begin this new day,
  Help us not to be like porridge,
Stiff and stodgy and slow to stir,
But like cornflakes,
Crisp and light and ready to serve.

L ord, as we begin this new day,
  Help us not to be like cornflakes,
Lightweight, brittle and cold,
But like porridge,
Warm, comforting and full of goodness.

Plaice, mackerel, haddock and cod,
these are the fish we eat, O God.
For prawns and shrimps, sardines on toast,
praise Father, Son and Holy Ghost.

Christopher Herbert

Thanks for breakfast, lunch and dinner,
If it weren't for you I'd be much thinner.

For bread and wine
And Auld Lang Syne,
God's holy name be praised.

Rub-a-dub-dub,
Thanks for the grub.

Thanks for chickens, thanks for eggs,
But why so many chicken legs . . .?
For custard creams and apple crumble,
Just bless the Lord and don't you grumble.

Historical
Graces

Historical graces ——————————

L ord Christ, we pray thy mercy on our table
   spread,
And what thy gentle hands have given thy men
Let it by thee be blessed.
Whatever we have came from thy lavish heart and
gentle hand,
And all that's good is thine, for thou art good.
And ye that eat, give thanks for it to Christ,
And let the words ye utter be only peace,
For Christ loved peace. It was himself that said,
Peace I give unto you, my peace I leave with you.
Grant that your own may be a generous hand
Breaking the bread for all poor men,
sharing the food.
Christ shall receive the bread thou gavest his poor,
And shall not tarry to give thee reward.

Alcuin of York (735-804)

To God who gives our daily bread
A thankful song we raise,
And pray that he who sends us food
ay fill our hearts with praise.

Thomas Tallis (c.1510-1585)

The eyes of all things do look up and trust in Thee; O Lord, thou givest them their meat in due season. Thou dost open thy hand and fillest with thy blessing everything living. Good Lord, bless us and all thy goods which we receive of thy bountiful liberality: Through Jesus Christ our Lord.

Queen Elizabeth I (1533-1603)

Historical graces

Thou that givest food to all flesh
which feed'st the young ravens that cry
unto thee
and hast nourished us from our youth up:
Fill our hearts with good and gladness
and establish our hearts with thy grace.

Lancelot Andrewes (1555-1626)

What God gives, and what we take,
'tis a gift for Christ his sake.
Be the meal of beans and peas,
God be thanked for those and these.
Have we flesh or have we fish,
All are fragments from his dish.
He his Church save, and the king,
and our peace here, like a spring,
make it ever flourishing.

Robert Herrick (1591-1674)

G od! To my little meal and oil
     Add but a bit of flesh to boil
And thou my pipkinnet shalt see
Give a wave-offering to thee.

Robert Herrick (1591-1674)

T hou who has given so much to me
    Give one thing more, a grateful heart,
for Christ's sake.

George Herbert (1593-1632)

M ost gracious God, who has given us Christ
    and with him all that is necessary to life
and godliness: we thankfully take this our food as
the gift of thy bounty, procured by his merits.
Bless it to the nourishment and strength of our
frail bodies to fit us for thy cheerful service.

Richard Baxter (1615-91)

Historical graces ───────

God send this crumb well down.

Prayer of a Royalist during the English Civil War

Lord, grant that whether I eat or drink, or whatever I do, I may do all to thy glory.

Thomas Ken (1637-1711)

Bless me, O Lord, and let my food strengthen me to serve thee, for Jesus Christ's sake.

Isaac Watts (1674-1748)

Be present at our table, Lord, Be here and everywhere adored Thy creatures bless and grant that we May feast in paradise with thee.

John Wesley (1703-92)

Thy providence supplies my food
And 'tis thy blessing makes it good.
My soul is nourished by thy word.
Let soul and body praise the Lord.

William Cowper (1731-1800)

For life and love, for rest and food,
For daily help and nightly care
Sing to the Lord for he is good,
And praise his name for it is fair.

J S B Monsell (1811-75)

Historical graces ───────────

A nd when thou art at thy meat, praise thy God:
In thought at ilke morsel and say thus in
thy heart:
Loved be thou king and thanked be thou king
and blessed be thou king.
Ihesu all my joying of all thy giftes good
that for me spilt thy blood and died on the rood.
Thou gave me grace to sing
the song of thy loving
my praise to thee ay spring
withouten any feigning.

The Lay Folks Mass Book

M ost loving Father, on whose bountiful
providence we do wholly depend:
Give us daily at thy pleasure whatsoever the
necessity of this life requireth:
but above all feed our souls with spiritual food,
with the bread of life from heaven:
through Jesus Christ our Lord.

*From Christian Prayers 1578 (after Eras-
mus)*

Graces for Children

Graces for children ───────

Bread is a lovely thing to eat –
  God bless the barley and the wheat;
A lovely thing to breathe is air –
God bless the sunshine everywhere;
The earth's a lovely place to know –
God bless the folks that come and go!
Alive's a lovely thing to be,
Giver of life – we say – bless thee!

For birds and beasts and bugs and bees,
  For fields and flowers and weeds and trees,
For schools and teachers, girls and boys,
Families, friends and crazy toys,
For love and laughter, food and fun,
We thank you, God, for every one.

Patrick Forbes

Here a little child I stand,
  Heaving up my either hand:
Cold as paddocks though they be,
Here I lift them up to Thee,
For a benison to fall
On our meat and on our all. Amen.

Robert Herrick (1591-1674)
('paddocks' are toads; a 'benison' is a blessing)

Our Father God, in whom we live,
  Accept the thanks thy children give,
Our needs are by thy bounty met,
May we the giver ne'er forget.

Robert Walmsley

Graces for children ─────────

For water-ices, cheap but good,
   that find us in a thirsty mood;
for ices made of milk or cream
that slip down smoothly as a dream;
for cornets, sandwiches and pies
that make the gastric juices rise;
for ices bought in little shops
or at the kerb from him who stops;
for chanting of the sweet refrain:
'chocolate, strawberry or plain?'
We thank thee, Lord, who sends with the heat
this cool deliciousness to eat.

Christopher Herbert

Graces by Children

Graces by children

G od is great, God is good,
Thank you, Lord, for all our food.

Traditional German children's grace

T hank you, Lord, for the food we eat,
for the clothes we wear,
for the games we play.
Help us never to forget those who have
little food to eat
and few clothes to wear, and no strength for
playing games.

F or my daily food, I thank you, Lord,
For the farmers, shopkeepers and cooks who
prepare my food, I thank you, Lord.
For my favourite foods, I thank you, Lord.
Help us to care about people not having enough
food. Amen.

Dear Lord Jesus, I'm sorry.
Sometimes I think about food too much.
I dream of all the delicious things there are to eat
when I really should be doing other things.
Please help me not to make food so important,
and help me not to be greedy at meal times. Amen.

Lord, bless this food and our family.

Nigel Nyumbu aged 12

Thank you, Lord, for this lovely food.

Miranda Nyumbu aged 4

Graces by children

G od, thank you for the food we eat each day
and help all the people around the world with
nothing but your love.

Ravitta Jisdhaul aged 11

M y prayer of thanksgiving for the food
we eat, Amen, Amen.
For the friends we have, Amen, Amen.
For the love you give us. Amen, Amen.

Michael Baird aged 9

D ear God, thank you for food
so we can be in a good mood,
And thank you for friends and family,
So we can all live happily. Amen.

Jessica Mistry aged 10

Dear God,
Thank you for the food you provide us with.
Bless all the animals who give us meat
and farmers who grow vegetables
so we have plenty to eat. Amen.

Kelly Devane aged 10

Thank you for our food,
Thank you for shops that sell us food.
Thank you for the water from the sky.
Thank you for being God. Amen.

Charlotte Franklin aged 8

Thank you for food and kindness,
Thank you for warmth and friends.
Thank you for trees and plants
And everything that gives us life. Amen.

Lee Simms aged 7

Graces by children

Dear God,
 Thank you for our food that we eat and
for drinks.
Please help all the other children and parents to
keep alive. Amen.

Hayley Reeves aged 7

Dear God,
 Thank you for our food that makes us
healthy and for the water that we drink and thank
you for giving us a family.
We are lucky to have a Mum and we are lucky to
have a God like you.

Dipesh Mistry aged 7

Dear God,
 Thank you for my home
and the rain and sun.
Thank you for my toys and food and fun.
Thank you for my school and all your gifts to me.
Thank you God for your generosity.

My dear loving God,
This prayer is to thank you for this special
world that I have been living in.
Thank you for your kindness and all your
gifts to us.
Thank you for our food and please help us to think
about other people who are hungry. Amen.

Tanya Walker aged 8

Dear God,
Thank you for food and drink,
Thank you for the way we think,
Thank you for flesh and meat,
Thank you for our arms and feet. Amen.

Nilesh Mistry aged 8

Graces by children

Dear God,
　　Thank you for giving us food, water, life
and animals.
Thank you for being our God,
Thank you for helping us. Amen.

Harinder Kaur aged 9

Dear Lord,
　　Thank you for our food and bless the hands
that make the food.
Bless us, O Lord, and thanks for all my friends
and my Mom and Dad.

Adam King aged 5

Dear Father God,
　　We thank you for our food and drink.
Thank you for sending the rain and the sun to
make the corn grow
so that the baker can make our bread and cakes.
Amen.

Anna Bennett aged 6

Dear Father God,
  Thank you for the food we eat especially the chips and hot dogs.
Thank you for the hot dog man who makes them for me. Amen.

Ajay Jilka aged 6

Dear God,
  Thank you for the cheese and peanut butter and jam for my sandwiches.

Adam Martin aged 5

Thank you, God, for all our food.
  Thank you for keeping the fisherman safe when they are at sea catching fish for my dinner. Amen.

Henry Miller aged 6

Graces by children

Dear Father God,
    Thank you for my Mummy who cleans my bedroom and cooks my tea. Amen.

James Marlow aged 5

Thank you, God, for our food and drink
    and our toys.
Thank you, God, for my friends who play with me.
Thank you for my Mummy and Daddy. Amen.

Christopher Halliwell aged 6

Graces from
Around the World

Graces from around the world —

Scotland

Some hae meat and canna eat.
And some wad eat that want it.
But we hae meat and we can eat
Ans sae the Lord be thankit.

Selkirk Grace
Robert Burns (1759-96)

No ordinary meal, a sacrament awaits us
On our table spread.
For men are risking lives on sea and land
That we may dwell in safety and be fed.

Doon head
Up paws
Thank God
We've jaws.

— Graces from around the world

Wales

O Arglwdd bendithia'n bwyd, i'n cadw'n fyw
i'th wasanaethu Di, drwy Iesu Grist. Amen.

O Lord, bless our food, that keeps us alive to serve
thee, through Jesus Christ our Lord. Amen.

John Parry

Graces from around the world —

Africa

God of my needfulness,
  grant me something to eat,
give me milk, give me sons,
give me herds, give me meat, O my Father.

African morning invocation

The bread is pure and fresh,
  The water cool and clear.
Lord of all life be with us,
Lord of all life be near.

O Lord, our meal is steaming before us and it
  smells very good. The water is clear and
fresh. We are happy and satisfied. But now we
think of our sisters and brothers all over the world
who have nothing to eat and only a little to drink.
Please, please through the help of their sisters and
brothers, let them have enough to eat and enough
to drink.

Prayer from West Africa

60

— Graces from around the world

Brazil

My God, I thank you for my food. It is you that allows the rice, the beans, the wheat, the fruit, the animals and the vegetables to grow. Thank you for the food that is on the table. Thank you very much.

Elizite Simon aged 11

China

Each time we eat, may we remember God's love.

Graces from around the world —

Egypt

O Lord, who fed the multitudes with five
barley loaves, bless what we are about to eat.

Germany

Come, Lord Jesus, be our guest,
and may our meal by you be blest.

*Traditional German grace attributed to
Martin Luther* (1483-1546)

Bless the food upon the dishes
as you blessed the loaves and fishes.
As the sugar's hid in the tea
So may our lives be hid in thee.

— Graces from around the world

Hawaii

Bless our home,
Father, that we cherish the bread before
there is none,
discover each other before we leave,
and enjoy each other for what we are, while we
have time.

India

For sharing your spirit with the whole
household of faith, that it may become your
new extended family with always room for more
around the table.
We thank you, good Father of us all.
Amen. So be it.

*Litany of thanksgiving for homes used in
Andrha Pradesh*

Graces from around the world —

O God above,
Make good for us all that we have cultivated.
Let it bear good fruit!
Let it be good fruit for us.
We shall eat new fruits.
Green mangoes, ripe mangoes, mophua, dates,
Let them be for our whole well being.
Deliver us from the tiger, the bear, the snake,
from all these venomous beasts:
Deliver us from all manner of disease
from suffering unto death,
and from all our enemies.

*Invocation used at the community eating of
the first-fruits among tribal people of the
Kond Hills in India*

— Graces from around the world

Switzerland

Because you are the Creator
and provider of everything,
Father God, as trusting children
do we pray to you
for our daily bread.

Strasbourg Hymnal

Praised be your loyalty,
You Father of all grace,
which today has blessed
us richly once again.

You give us at all times
here on earth our daily bread.
O bless us with peace
In life and in death.

R Wimmer

Graces from around the world —

Y ou present us, God, so fatherly
  now food and drink: we praise you,
because everything which nourishes and
strengthens us,
is given by your hand.

Sixteenth century prayer printed on a
serviette in a Swiss hotel

W ith every bite we eat
   We do not want to forget to give thanks.
Whatever brings us your blessing
shall be to the glory of your name.
Give thanks to the Lord because he is kind
and his goodness will last forever.
Now let us give to God the Lord thanks,
and give him glory
for all his gifts which we have received.

Ludwig Helmbold

— *Graces from around the world*

United States of America

God of grace,
  sustain our bodies with this food,
our hearts with true friendship
and our souls with your truth, for Christ's sake.
Amen.

Lord Jesus, be our holy guest,
  our morning joy, our evening rest;
and with our daily bread impart
your love and peace to every heart. Amen

Graces from around the world ——

B lessed are you, Lord.
You have fed us from the earliest days.
You give food to every living creature.
Fill our hearts with joy and delight.
Let us always have enough and something to spare
for works of mercy
In honour of Christ Jesus, our Lord.

Through him may glory, honour and power be
yours forever. Amen.

T he eyes of all wait upon you, O Lord,
and you give them their food in due season.
You open your hand
And fill all living things with plenteousness.
Amen.

Graces for
Special Occasions

Graces for special occasions ───

Weddings

For the joys of meeting, greeting and eating.
We give you thanks.

Bishop Gavin Reid

For all this day's reminders
That you are a God of love.
We give you thanks. Amen.

Bishop Gavin Reid

Heavenly Father, God of love,
thank you for the gift of marriage which we
celebrate today.
Thank you for this marvellous wedding feast
spread before us and for the friends and family
gathered here to share it.
Bless us now as we eat, and particularly bless
(John and Mary) in their new life together. May
every meal time be as happy for them as this.
Amen.

Harvest

We thank thee now, O Father
for all things bright and good
The seed time and the harvest
Our life, our health, our food.
No gifts have we to offer
For all thy love imparts
But that which thou desirest
Our humble, grateful hearts.

All good gifts around us
Are sent from heaven above.
Then thank the Lord,
O thank the Lord
For all his love.

Matthias Claudius (1740-1815)

Graces for special occasions ———

We dare not ask you bless our harvest feast
  'til it is spread for poorest and for least,
We dare not bring our harvest gifts to you
Unless our hungry brothers share them too.

Not only at this time, Lord, every day
Those whom you love are dying while we pray,
Teach us to do with less, and so to share
From our abundance more than we can spare.

Now with this harvest plenty round us piled,
Show us the Christ in every starving child;
Speak, as you spoke of old in Galilee,
'You feed, or you refuse, not them but me'.

Lilian Cox

——— *Graces for special occasions*

Birthdays

For friends and presents,
  Birthday cake and candles,
Balloons and parties and friends to share them all,
A year gone by and a new year to look forward to,
we thank you, Lord.

Picnics

For the sandwiches, fruit, crisps and cakes
  Spread out here upon the grass *(or sand)*,
Even for the insects which want to share it with us,
We thank you, Lord.
It is a privilege to eat your gifts of fresh food here
in the fresh air of your creation.

Graces for special occasions ——

Lent

Instead of living it up
  Try giving it up . . . for Lent.
Chocolates, sweets, a glass of beer,
Swearing, eating to excess . . .
And then spend what you save to bless
The poor.
Give thanks to God for all he gives,
For Christ, once dead, now lives!

Patrick Forbes

——— Graces for special occasions

Easter

On this Easter day we thank you that you gave
your life to save us from our sin,
We thank you that you rose from the dead to give
us life,
and we thank you that each new day you give us
our daily bread.

Pam Robertson

The yeast in the hot cross buns transforms the
dough and makes them rise.
Lord, whenever we see these familiar symbols of
your glorious resurrection during this season of
Eastertide, help us to remember how you
transformed the world by rising victorious on
Easter day.
Amen.

Graces for special occasions ———

Christmas

Thank you for our food this day and thank you for the reminder that Christ the Saviour of mankind is born. Amen.

For holly's cheerful crimson berry,
For children's faces shining merry,
For all our loved ones gathered here,
For absent loved ones far and near,
For food to hearten us in eating,
For wine to gladden us in drinking,
For love, for health, for happiness,
For joy and faith and hope of peace,
For countless other gifts beside,
We thank thee, Lord, this Christmastide.

A Women's Institute Christmas grace

Musical Graces

Musical graces

Praise God from whom all blessings flow,
Praise Him all creatures here below,
Praise Him above the heavenly host.
Praise Father, Son and Holy Ghost.

Thomas Ken (1637-1711)

The Lord is good to me,
And so I thank the Lord
For giving me the things I need
The sun, the rain and the appleseed.
The Lord is good to me.

And every seed that grows
Will grow into a tree.
And one day soon
Therc'll be apples there,
For everyone in the world to share,
The Lord is good to me.

'Johnny Appleseed grace'
John Chapman (1774-1845)

Musical graces ————————————————

We thank you, Lord, for daily food,
and every other thing that's good:
music and art and friends to share
the gift of life in every mood.

But who can handle every mood,
save he who gives us daily food,
the Lord who hears and answers prayer,
and holds us firm for all that's good?

So, Lord, we praise you, wholly good,
and seek your help in every mood
to show our neighbours proper care,
and share with all our daily food.

Jock Stein

Musical graces

Here is our food and we'll share it out among us all,
Gathered from north, south, west and east;
And we'll sing as we eat with Jesus in our company,
'Who'll come and share in the kingdom feast?'

We're on a journey, we're on a journey,
We're on a journey, a faith pilgrimage,
And we'll sing as we eat with Jesus in our company,
'Who'll come and share in the kingdom feast?'

Jock Stein

Musical graces

83

Musical graces

Thank you for the world so sweet,
Thank you for the food we eat,
Thank you for the birds that sing,
Thank you, God, for everything.

E Rutter Leatham

Thank you for the world so sweet, Thank you for the food we eat,
Thank you for the birds that sing, Thank you, God, for ev- ery-thing.

For health and strength and daily food,
we praise your name, O God.

May be sung as a 4-part round

For health and strength and dai- ly food we
praise your name O God.

Latin Graces

Latin graces

Dominus Jesus, sit potus et esus.

Lord Jesus, be drink and food.

Martin Luther (1483-1546)

Benedic, Domine, nobis et his donis tuis, quae tua gratia et munificentia sumus iam sumpturi; et concede ut illis salubriter a te nutriti tibi debitum obsequium praestare valeamus per Christum Dominum nostrum. Amen.

Lord, bless us and these thy gifts which with thy grace and bounty we are now to eat; and grant that, nourished therewith by thee to our health, we may honour thee with the praise which we owe thee, through Christ our Lord. Amen.

King's College, Cambridge

Index of authors and sources

Index of first lines

For these gifts of food, 11
For valour – a phrase so short, 23
For water ices, cheap but good, 46
For well-filled plate, 31
For what we are about to receive, 10

God bless this bunch, 30
God is great, God is good, 48
God of grace, sustain our bodies with this food, 67
God of my needfulness, 60
God save the King, 21
God send this crumb well down, 40
God, thank you for the food we eat, 50
God! To my little meal and oil, 39
God, you give good things liberally, 14
God, we thank you for this food, 8
Gracious God, may the food that we are about to receive,
   13

Heavenly Father, God of love, 70
Heavenly Father, We thank you for our homes, 11
Here a little child I stand, 45
Here is our food, 82

I'm ready for it, Lord, 30

Instead of living it up, 74
In thanks to God for all his benefits,
In giving you thanks for this food, 11

Lord, as we begin this new day, 32
Lord, bless this food, 49
Lord, bless us and these thy gifts, 86
Lord Christ, we pray thy mercy on our table spread, 36
Lord, for these and all your gifts, 9

On this Easter day we thank you, 75
Our Father God, in whom we live, 45

Plaice, mackerel, haddock and cod, 33
Praise God from whom all blessings flow, 78
Praised be your loyalty, 65

Rub-a-dub-dub, 34

Some hae meat and canna eat, 58

Thank God for dirty dishes, 26
Thank you for food and kindness, 51
Thank you for our food, 51
Thank you for our food this day, 76
Thank you for the world so sweet, 84
Thank you, God, for all our food, 55
Thank you, God, for our food and drink, 56
Thank you, Lord, for the food we eat, 48
Thank you, Lord, for this lovely food, 49
Thank you, Lord, for this Mess, 20
Thanks for breakfast, lunch and dinner, 33
Thanks for chickens, thanks for eggs, 34
The bread is pure and fresh, 60
The eyes of all things do look up and trust in thee, 37
The eyes of all wait upon you, O Lord, 68
The Lord is good to me, 79
The yeast in the hot cross buns, 75
This is the day the Lord has made, 31
Thou that givest food to all flesh, 38
Thou who hast given so much to me, 39
Thy providence supplies my food, 41
To God who gives our daily bread, 37

We break the bread of brotherhood, 8

We dare not ask you bless our harvest feast, 72
We have food while others are starving, 12
We thank thee now O Father, 71
We thank you, Lord, for daily food, 80
What God gives, and what we take, 38
With every bite we eat, 66

You present us, God, 66

Index of occasions and subjects

ACKNOWLEDGEMENTS

The compiler and publisher gratefully acknowledge permission to reproduce copyright material in this anthology. Every effort has been made to trace and contact copyright holders. If there are any inadvertent omissions we apologise to those concerned.

Curtis Brown: from *Words for Worship*, edited by Campling and Davis, 14, 15. Cassells: from *The Prayer Manual*, 16. The Reverend Patrick Forbes, 23, 27, 44, 74. The Girl Guides of Canada: *World Hunger Grace* by the Hunger Task Force, Anglican Church Diocese of Huron, 28. HarperCollins Publishers Ltd.: from *Short Prayers for the Long Day* compiled by Giles and Melville Harcourt, 14 and from *Prayers for Children* by Elizabeth Laird, 48. The Venerable Christopher Herbert, 24, 25, 33, 46. Hodder & Stoughton: from *A Treasury of Prayer* edited by Tony Castle, 13 and *A Patchwork Prayer* by Janet Lynch-Watson, 49. The Reverend H Ingamells, 30, 31. Kingsway Publications: from *Prayers for Today's Church* © 1972 Dick Williams, 11. David W Lankshear, 12. Lion Publishing: from *365 Children's Prayers*, 49. The Liturgical Press, Collegeville, Minnesota: from *The Pilgrim's Guide to the Holy Land* by Stephen Doyle © 1985 The Order of St Benedict, Inc., 15. The Lutheran World Federation, 61. Mowbrays: from *Prayers for Use at the Alternative Services*, edited by David Silk, 14. Oxford University Press: from *The Oxford Book of Prayer* edited by George Appleton, 13. Bishop Gavin Reid, 70. Pam Robertson, 10, 75. The Scout Association, London: from *Scout Prayers*, 28. Helena Smalman-Smith, 70, 73, 75. SPCK: from *Another Day* compiled by J Carden, 60, 63 and *A Little Book of Prayers* by Lilian Cox, 72. Audrey Stanley, 10. Jock Stein, 80, 82. United Nations Music Publishing: for a tune © 1972 Jimmy Owen, 78. The Westminster Press, Philadelphia, from *Daily Prayer: The Worship of God*, 67, 68.

THE NATIONAL SOCIETY

A Christian Voice in Education

The National Society (Church of England) for Promoting Religious Education is a charity which supports all those involved in Christian education – teachers and school governors, students and parents, clergy and lay people – with the resources of its RE centres, archives, courses and conferences.

Founded in 1811, the Society was chiefly responsible for setting up the nationwide network of Church schools in England and Wales and still provides grants for building projects and legal and administrative advice for headteachers and governors. It now publishes a wide range if books, pamphlets and audio-visual items, and two magazines, *Crosscurrent* and *Together*.

For details of membership of the Society or to receive a copy of our current catalogue please contact:

> The Promotions Secretary,
> The National Society,
> Church House,
> Great Smith Street,
> London
> SW1P 3NZ
> Telephone: 071-222 1672